551

Wood W9-ASD-996

Earthquakes.

EARTHQUAKES

MICHAEL WOODS AND MARY B. WOODS

Sheboygan Falls Schools
Middle School Library
Sheboygan Falls, WI 53085

LERNER PUBLICATIONS COMPANY
MINNEAPOLIS

To Alexander Charles Woods

Editor's note: Determining the exact death toll following disasters is often difficult—if not impossible—especially in the case of disasters that took place long ago. The authors and the editors in this series have used their best judgment in determining which figures to include.

Text copyright © 2007 by Michael Woods and Mary B. Woods

All rights reserved. International copyright secured. No part of this book may be reproduced, stored in a retrieval system, or transmitted in any form or by any means—electronic, mechanical, photocopying, recording, or otherwise—without the prior written permission of Lerner Publishing Group, except for the inclusion of brief quotations in an acknowledged review.

Lerner Publications Company
A division of Lerner Publishing Group
241 First Avenue North
Minneapolis, MN 55401 U.S.A.

Website address: www.lernerbooks.com

Library of Congress Cataloging-in-Publication Data

Woods, Michael, 1946–
    Earthquakes / by Michael Woods and Mary B. Woods.
        p.   cm. — (Disasters up close)
    Includes bibliographical references and index.
    ISBN-13: 978–0–8225–4711–2 (lib. bdg. : alk. paper)
    ISBN-10: 0–8225–4711–2 (lib. bdg. : alk. paper)
    1. Earthquakes—Juvenile literature. I. Woods, Mary B. (Mary Boyle), 1946–
II. Title. III. Series.
QE521.3.W676 2007
363.34'95—dc22   2005032491

Manufactured in the United States of America
1 2 3 4 5 6 – DP – 12 11 10 09 08 07

Contents

Introduction

LISHBA, AGE FIVE, WAS AT HOME WATCHING TELEVISION ON OCTOBER 8, 2005. LISHBA AND HER FAMILY LIVE IN KASHMIR, A REGION IN SOUTH ASIA. KASHMIR IS DIVIDED BETWEEN THE COUNTRIES OF INDIA AND PAKISTAN. SUDDENLY, THE HOUSE BEGAN TO SHAKE. "I GOT SCARED AND RAN TO MY FATHER," LISHBA SAID.

Lishba's father knew the shaking came from an earthquake. He feared that their house would fall down on top of them. So the family ran outside into the yard. When people tried to walk, they tipped from side to side, as if they were on a boat in wavy water. Across Kashmir, houses and buildings—including Lishba's home—began to collapse.

TRAPPED IN THE RUBBLE

"I heard a blast," a policeman named Karam Umrani remembered. He was near a tall apartment building in the city of Islamabad, Pakistan, when the quake began.

The building fell to the ground. "I heard the cries of the people trapped inside there," Karam said. "I could do only one thing, which was to pick people out of the rubble, and with my bare hands I started to dig."

In the hours and days after the earthquake struck, hundreds of victims were pulled from the rubble across Kashmir. They often had broken bones, head injuries, and other serious medical problems. Some victims lived in the mountains, far away from hospitals or doctors. Survivors also had another problem—the quake had left more than 3 million people homeless.

Houses in Batagram, Pakistan, lay in ruins following the massive 2005 quake.

HELPING HANDS

Rescue workers from around the world came to help the people in Kashmir. They brought food, tents for shelter, and medicine. But the workers had trouble bringing relief to everyone who needed it. Some villages could only be reached by helicopter, and there weren't enough helicopters to do the job.

In November 2005, winter weather arrived in Kashmir. Life became even more difficult. A Pakistani farmer said, "My family needs a roof over their heads. . . . I do not know what [we should] do when the snow falls."

The October quake had lasted just 60 seconds. In that short time, however, it caused a great disaster. It killed more than 80,000 people and injured 128,000. Major earthquakes—the kind that cause big disasters—are rare, but somewhere on Earth, an earthquake takes place every single day.

"Suddenly the walls turned to jelly."

—Jan Peter Stellema, witness to the 2005 South Asia earthquake

A survivor of the October, 2005, earthquake in Kashmir searches the rubble for bodies of relatives.

When the Earth Quakes

EARTHQUAKES ARE A SHAKING OF EARTH'S SURFACE. THEY OCCUR WHEN LAYERS OF UNDERGROUND ROCK SUDDENLY CHANGE POSITION.

When the ground shakes, everything attached to it also shakes. That includes buildings, bridges, and roads. Earthquakes can make these structures crack, break apart, or collapse. The shaking may also damage tunnels, pipes, and wires buried in the ground.

Earthquakes are among the most terrible disasters in the world. Disasters are events that cause great destruction. Strong earthquakes may release ten thousand times more energy than a powerful bomb. They destroy whole cities and kill thousands of people.

ONE DISASTER LEADS TO ANOTHER

Earthquakes sometimes set off other disasters. Quakes under the ocean can cause tsunamis. These enormous waves can be more than 100 feet (30 meters) high and travel as fast as a jet plane. They crash onto coasts, smashing buildings and causing floods. In 2004 a huge earthquake struck under the Indian Ocean. It produced tsunamis that hit a dozen countries in southern Asia and eastern Africa. The waves killed more than 150,000 people and injured 500,000.

KILLER CAVES

Earthquakes don't kill people. Buildings do. Most earthquake injuries and deaths happen when objects fall on people or trap them in collapsing buildings.

In 1556 an earthquake struck an area of central China where people lived in caves. The caves collapsed, trapping people inside. About 830,000 people were killed, making it the deadliest recorded earthquake.

The large waves from the 2004 Indian Ocean tsunami—which was the result of an earthquake—carried a vehicle onto the top of this building. It is in the Banda Aceh Province of Indonesia, which was the area hardest hit by the tsunami.

Landslides occur when earthquakes shake soil and rock loose from the sides of hills. A 1994 quake in Northridge, California, produced thousands of landslides. They buried houses, blocked roads, and snapped power lines.

Earthquakes can also spark fires when they break natural gas pipes and cut power lines. And if the quake has damaged water pipes, firefighters have no way to stop the flames. After the great 1906 San Francisco, California, earthquake, fire destroyed much of the city.

"With no water to fight it, the great fire raged for three days and three nights," Charles Kendrick recalled. "When the sea of flames finally died down, some of the burned-over areas smoldered for weeks. The wilderness of ruins was beyond words—thousands of blocks of complete desolation."

ON SHAKY GROUND

Sometimes earthquakes swallow whole buildings. When an earthquake shakes wet ground, the tiny pieces of soil may come apart. Then the soil turns soft. Scientists call it liquefied soil. Houses and other buildings resting on the soil suddenly have nothing firm to stand on. The unstable ground may cause them to fall over, or it may swallow them up.

A WHOLE LOT OF SHAKIN'

Earthquakes are very common. As many as 3.3 million earthquakes occur around the world every year. That's 9,000 each day! Most are so small that nobody notices them. Scientists can detect about 500,000 quakes a year, and people can feel about 100,000.

Nearly 7,000 earthquakes each year are strong enough to cause some damage. It's usually minor, with small objects falling off tables and shelves. About 18 major earthquakes take place each year.

Big quakes that occur where few people live may cause little or no damage. When major earthquakes occur near cities, millions of people may be affected.

A 1972 earthquake in Managua, Nicaragua, leveled much of the city.

"*My first thought of downtown was of a bomb attack* as I had remembered from high school textbook pictures of *World War II.*"

—Gail Meighan, after the 1972 earthquake in Managua, Nicaragua

This illustration shows the quaking of the ground and sea during the Lisbon quake.

November 1, 1755
LISBON, PORTUGAL

At 9:29 A.M. on November 1, 1755, Lisbon's 275,000 residents were enjoying a sunny morning in the coastal city. Many were in church, celebrating the Christian holiday All Saints' Day. One minute later, a great earthquake rumbled through the ground. It killed as many as 90,000 people and almost destroyed one of the world's most beautiful cities.

Scientists say the 1755 Lisbon earthquake was one of the strongest ever documented. It may have been 9.0 on the Richter scale, a modern measurement of an earthquake's strength.

Thousands of survivors of the earthquake immediately rushed to the Lisbon harbor. The harbor had no tall buildings that could collapse, so people thought it was safe. Some residents thought that ships in the harbor were even safer, and they crowded on board. As it turned out, the harbor was one of the worst places to be.

The massive Lisbon earthquake caused tsunamis and a terrible fire.

Next came a tsunami, a wall of water 50 feet (15 meters) high. It had formed in the nearby Atlantic Ocean because of the quake. It rushed up the Tagus River, which flows through Lisbon into the ocean. The water roared through 0.5 mile (0.8 km) of Lisbon. It swept up debris and people and carried them out to sea. Other tsunamis generated by the quake also caused great damage along the coasts of Spain and nearby Africa. They even swept across the Atlantic Ocean and to islands in the Caribbean Sea 3,400 miles (5,500 km) away.

Charles Davy was an eyewitness. *"It came on foaming and roaring, and rushed towards the shore with such impetuosity, that we all immediately ran for our lives as fast as possible,"* he wrote. *"Many were actually swept away, and the rest above their waist in water."* He survived only by holding onto a heavy object as the tsunami tried to suck him out to sea.

In areas of the city that escaped the tsunami, fires broke out. The quake's shaking had toppled church candles and cooking fires. The fires burned for three days, causing even more damage and destruction.

> *In an instant there appeared a large body of water, rising as it were like a mountain.*
> —Charles Davy, eyewitness to the Lisbon quake

What Causes Earthquakes

EARTHQUAKES HAPPEN BECAUSE EARTH'S OUTER SHELL, OR CRUST, IS NOT SOLID. IT'S BROKEN UP INTO ENORMOUS CHUNKS OF FLOATING ROCK CALLED TECTONIC PLATES. EACH PLATE IS ABOUT 50 MILES (80 KM) THICK.

Earth's surface has seven big plates and many smaller ones. Below them is a layer of hot, semisolid (molten) rock called magma. The plates float on the molten rock like a leaf in a puddle of water. North America and the other continents ride on top of the plates. So do the world's oceans. The plates are constantly moving.

PLATES AND SHAKES

To talk about Earth's plates and their movements, scientists use the theory of plate tectonics. This theory explains how earthquakes happen and where we can expect to see them again.

Tectonic plates fit together like the pieces of a jigsaw puzzle. When one plate pushes against another plate, stress builds up. The stress causes faults, or cracks, in the crust. Faults often develop deep underground. A few can be seen on the surface. One of the most famous is California's San Andreas Fault.

As more stress builds up underground, layers of rock suddenly slip. The movement releases the built-up stress and shakes the ground above.

This map shows Earth's major tectonic plates.

NORTH AMERICAN PLATE

EURASIAN PLATE

JUAN DE FUCA PLATE

CARIBBEAN PLATE

ARABIAN PLATE

INDIAN PLATE

PACIFIC PLATE

PHILIPPINE PLATE

COCOS PLATE

AFRICAN PLATE

PACIFIC PLATE

NAZCA PLATE

SOUTH AMERICAN PLATE

AUSTRALIAN PLATE

SCOTIA PLATE

ANTARCTIC PLATE

California's San Andreas Fault is about 600 miles (970 km) long. The fault forms part of the boundary between the Pacific and North American plates.

The stress is often greatest along plate boundaries. That's exactly where most earthquakes take place.

Scientists have identified three main types of plate boundaries, based on how the plates are moving. Keep in mind that plates don't move smoothly. The sudden jerks and bumps of plate movement are the reason we have earthquakes.

Divergent boundaries are where plates are moving apart. Magma flows up between the plates, pushing them away from one another. When the magma cools and hardens, it forms new crust.

FAST AS A FINGERNAIL

How fast do the giant plates of rock in Earth's surface move? To get an idea, watch your fingernails. Fingernails in young people grow about 2 to 3 inches (5 to 8 centimeters) a year. Slow tectonic plates move about 1 inch (2.5 cm) per year. The fastest travel about 6 inches (15 cm) each year.

Convergent boundaries are where two or more plates are coming together. When two plates carrying continents come together, the crust piles up, forming mountains. When a plate carrying a continent meets a plate carrying an ocean, the oceanic plate slips underneath the other plate. It slowly sinks down into the magma. As the sinking plate melts, crust is destroyed.

Transform boundaries are where two plates slide past each other. Crust is neither produced nor destroyed.

FINDING FAULTS

Many of the world's earthquakes occur along the Ring of Fire. This band stretches around the Pacific Ocean. Tectonic plates meet all around the edges of the Pacific Ocean, causing quakes on all sides.

Because faults are likely to appear anywhere that two or more plates meet, earthquakes are not limited to the Ring of Fire. Turkey, for example, has frequent quakes. They happen because Turkey sits on the small Anatolian plate. It is being squeezed between three big tectonic plates—the African, Arabian, and Eurasian. Movement by any one of these plates pushes the Anatolian plate and causes a quake in Turkey.

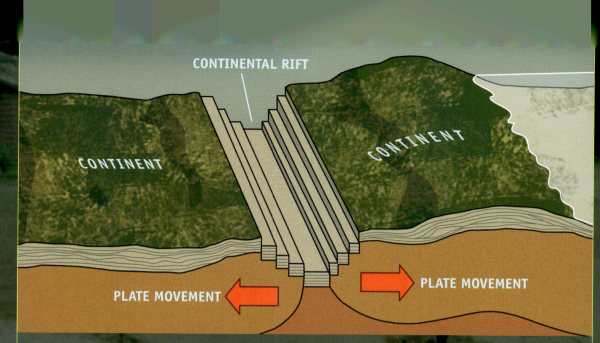

CONTINENTAL RIFT

CONTINENT

CONTINENT

PLATE MOVEMENT

PLATE MOVEMENT

AT THIS DIVERGENT BOUNDARY, two tectonic plates are moving apart. The low area between the two plates is called a continental rift. Divergent boundaries are also found in the ocean.

CONVERGENT BOUNDARIES

OCEAN

TRENCH

CONTINENT

MOUNTAINS

CONTINENT

PLATE

MOVEMENT

AT CONVERGENT BOUNDARIES, two tectonic plates push into each other. When both plates carry continents *(right)*, the pushing causes the crust to crumple up, forming mountains. When one of the plates carries an ocean *(left)*, the oceanic plate slides under the continental plate. This causes an ocean trench to form.

15

Some earthquakes happen along faults far away from plate boundaries. One example is the New Madrid Fault in Missouri. This fault is in the middle of the North American plate.

The rock around mid-plate faults is different from the rock at plate boundaries. Underground rock at the edges of tectonic plates is hot and flexible. When plates slip, the rock flexes (bends) and absorbs some of the energy from the plate movement. But underground rock near faults in the middle of tectonic plates is cold and hard. It does not flex much. When sections of the fault slip, more energy travels through the ground, causing greater damage over a larger area.

ROCK AND ROLL

Sudden slips of rock below Earth's surface make vibrations, or waves, in the ground. These rocky ripples are just like the ripples from a stone thrown into a pool of water. They are called seismic waves. They cause the shaking people feel during an earthquake.

Seismic waves spread out from the hypocenter, the underground point where the fault began to slip. An earthquake's epicenter is the point on the surface directly above the hypocenter.

MY DOG HAS FLEAS!

People in ancient times didn't know what caused earthquakes. They told myths and legends to explain why the ground shook. These stories described such creatures as giant spiders, snakes, turtles, and ants that lived deep underground.

In India people believed that elephants held up the earth. The elephants' movements caused earthquakes. People in Siberia, Russia, said the earth rested on a sled pulled by dogs with fleas. When the dogs scratched at the fleas, the earth shook. In ancient Greece, people thought that strong winds blowing through underground tunnels shook the earth.

The 1994 Northridge quake in California measured 6.4 on the Richter scale. The violent shaking damaged many highways and bridges.

"I truly thought I was going to die. I've never been so frightened in my life."

—LeAnne Katz, after the 1994 Northridge, California, earthquake

The epicenter, however, isn't always the point of heaviest damage. Faults can be many miles long. And seismic waves shake areas all along the fault. Places close to the fault usually have more damage than those farther away. But they may be some distance from the epicenter. If the epicenter is in the wilderness, for example, damage may be much greater in distant cities with more people and buildings.

This apartment building was at risk of collapsing after the 1989 Loma Prieta quake in northern California.

Earthquakes produce two main types of seismic waves, body waves and surface waves. Body waves travel below Earth's surface through the inside, or body, of rock layers. They can speed through Earth at 2 to 4 miles per second (3 to 6 km/s). The first shaking that people feel from an earthquake comes from body waves. They make buildings and other structures shake from side to side.

Surface waves move much more slowly along the surface of the ground. They follow body waves. Sometimes people can see surface waves roll across the ground like waves on the ocean. Surface waves cause the most damage to buildings, roads, underground pipes, and other structures.

FEEL THE WAVES

Seismic waves travel great distances. People can feel an earthquake hundreds of miles away from the epicenter. But the waves get weaker as they move away from the epicenter. Seismic waves from an 1811 earthquake in New Madrid, Missouri, uprooted trees. When the waves reached New York City and Boston, Massachusetts, they had only enough strength to knock books off shelves.

Seismic waves also carry a message about an earthquake's location. Since body waves and surface waves travel at different speeds, scientists can measure the time between the two types of waves to calculate how far away the epicenter is. The longer the time between the waves, the farther away the epicenter is.

A California highway buckled during a
1992 earthquake. The yellow line on
either side of the crack shows how far
the road shifted

1811–1812
NEW MADRID, MISSOURI

These trees were nearly uprooted by the New Madrid earthquakes.

Mother Nature rang an alarm clock for hundreds of people in New Madrid, Missouri, on December 16, 1811. At about 2 A.M., a powerful earthquake shook everyone out of bed. One eyewitness said, **"We were awakened by a most tremendous noise. . . . The house danced about and seemed as if it would fall on our heads."** Frightened people ran into the streets in their pajamas and nightgowns. They tottered from side to side as waves rolled through the ground like swells on the ocean.

Eliza Bryan remembered an awful noise like thunder. She smelled an odor that stunk of rotten eggs coming from cracks in the ground. She wrote, **"The screams of the affrighted inhabitants running to and fro, not knowing where to go, or what to do—the cries of the fowls and beasts of every species—the cracking of trees falling, and the roaring of the Mississippi [River] . . . formed a scene truly horrible."**

20

A landslide following the New Madrid earthquakes created rough terrain in the Chickasaw Bluffs in Tennessee.

In the months that followed, thousands of smaller quakes, or aftershocks, shook the central and eastern United States. Two more big quakes hit New Madrid on January 23, 1812, and on February 7, 1812. They were strong enough to cause church bells to ring 700 miles (1,130 km) away in Washington, D.C.

If we do not get away from here the ground is going to eat us alive.

—George Heinrich Crist

The New Madrid earthquakes swallowed up houses, barns, and five entire towns in three states. Some areas of the ground buckled up, forming hills 50 feet (15 meters) high. Other areas dropped so that treetops were even with the ground. Islands in the Mississippi River disappeared. In one area of Tennessee, the Mississippi River briefly flowed *backward* into a caved-in area of ground. It formed Reelfoot Lake, which people still call Earthquake Lake.

The quakes affected about 1 million square miles (2,590,000 square km). The strongest shaking occurred in Missouri, Tennessee, Kentucky, Indiana, Illinois, Ohio, Alabama, Arkansas, and Mississippi. But people from the Rocky Mountains to the Atlantic coast and from Canada to Mexico felt the tremors from these major quakes.

Reelfoot Lake formed after an 1812 earthquake in New Madrid.

21

Earthquake Country

CALIFORNIA AND OTHER WESTERN STATES ARE KNOWN AS EARTHQUAKE COUNTRY. MOST AMERICANS THINK THAT THE WESTERN HALF OF THE UNITED STATES IS THE ONLY AREA WHERE EARTHQUAKES ARE A THREAT. STRONG QUAKES DO OCCUR MOST OFTEN IN WESTERN STATES. BUT EARTHQUAKES HAPPEN IN ALL FIFTY STATES AND ALL U.S. TERRITORIES. FORTY-ONE STATES AND TERRITORIES HAVE A MODERATE OR HIGH RISK OF EARTHQUAKES.

Debris from a 2001 Seattle, Washington, earthquake crushed this van.

Alaska experiences more big earthquakes than any other state. Many Alaskan earthquakes happen in wilderness areas where few people live. Although strong, they cause little damage. California has the most earthquakes that cause damage. California has a high population and lots of big cities. When a strong quake hits California, it's more likely to topple buildings and injure people.

Earthquakes in the eastern half of the United States are rare but very dangerous. The strongest earthquakes ever in the continental United States occurred in Missouri in the 1800s.

THE NEXT BIG ONE

Some scientists think the next big U.S. quake could strike the eastern United States. Before the year 2050, they predict a 90 percent chance of a strong eastern shaker like the 1811–1812 New Madrid, Missouri, earthquakes. Millions of people live in the East. Such a quake could be a serious disaster.

THE RING OF FIRE

About 80 percent of the world's big earthquakes occur in a belt that stretches around the Pacific Ocean. Scientists call it the Ring of Fire because many volcanoes also erupt in the region. This big earthquake belt goes northward from Chile (in South America) to California to Alaska. Then it continues westward to Japan and the Philippine Islands and finally south to New Zealand.

CRACKS IN THE CRUST

Faults zigzag over Earth's surface like cracks in the shell of a hard-boiled egg. In the United States, the San Andreas Fault in California is the most famous of these earthquake-prone zones.

Another well-known U.S. fault is the New Madrid Fault, which is about 150 miles (241 km) long. It runs through Arkansas, Missouri, Tennessee, Kentucky, and Illinois. The Denali Fault runs for more than 1,200 miles (1,931 km) through Alaska and northwestern Canada.

Worldwide, major faults include the North Anatolian Fault in Turkey, the Alpine Fault on New Zealand's South Island, and the Atacama Fault in Chile.

EARTHQUAKE COUNTRIES

Between 1900 and 2005, Iran had 17 earthquakes that killed at least 1,000 people each, more than any other country. China had 13; Turkey, 12; Japan, 9; India, 8; Italy, 6; and Pakistan, 1. The United States had only the 1906 San Francisco quake.

Pakistani men pray in front of the destroyed mosque (Islamic house of worship) in Balakot after the devastating quake that rocked the region in 2005.

23

DISASTER ZONES

Many of the world's earthquakes are located along the Ring of Fire.
This map shows where some of Earth's major quakes have taken place.
The boxed information describes especially destructive earthquakes.

IZMIT—Turkey
1999 (20,000+ deaths)

BAM—Iran
2003 (26,000+ deaths)

ASIA

KOBE—Japan
1995 (6,400+
deaths)

EUROPE

SPITAK—
Armenia

SOUTH ASIA
2005 (80,000+ deaths)

TANGSHAN—China

KANTO—
Japan

MESSINA—Italy

LISBON—Portugal
1775 (90,000 deaths)

BHUJ—India

GUJARAT
STATE—
India

SHENSHI
PROVINCE—China
1556
(830,000+deaths)

HAICHENG—China

AFRICA

SUMATRA—Indonesia

AUSTRALIA

ALASKA—U.S.A.

SAN FRANCISCO—U.S.A.
1906 (3,000 deaths)

NORTH AMERICA

SANTA BARBARA—U.S.A.

NEW MADRID—U.S.A.

NORTHRIDGE—U.S.A.

MEXICO CITY—Mexico
1985 (9,500+ deaths)

PORT ROYAL—Jamaica

MANAGUA—Nicaragua

PACIFIC OCEAN

SOUTH AMERICA

CHILE
1960 (2,000 deaths)

April 18, 1906
SAN FRANCISCO, CALIFORNIA

Much of San Francisco burned to the ground after the famous 1906 earthquake.

In 1906 one of the world's most famous earthquakes struck. The great San Francisco earthquake was estimated to be 8.25 on the Richter scale.

The shaking started at 5:12 A.M. and lasted less than one minute. But it killed approximately 2,500 people and caused at least $400 million in damage. Hundreds of people were trapped under piles of bricks and broken wood when buildings collapsed.

Charles B. Sedgwick, a newspaper editor, remembered one wrecked building near the corner of Second and Stevenson streets. *"Two firemen were wearily pitching bricks from the heap, and a woman standing near called out to me: 'Go over and help them, mister. There are people buried there.' 'They must be dead,' I said. 'No,' she replied, 'they are not all dead, for we hear them groan. There must be twenty there.'"*

A half dozen other people also hurried to help. *"We all worked in silence, nobody speaking a word,"*

Sedgwick remembered. **"Soon the firemen were called away, and the rest of us . . . stopped."** They realized their work was hopeless and left. Fire was spreading through the city, and the survivors had to flee if they hoped to escape.

The quake had cracked underground pipes that carried natural gas. People used the gas for cooking and to light their homes at night. As gas leaked out, it caught fire. The quake had also broken water pipes. Firefighters did not have enough water to fight the flames.

Crowds of people who lost their homes fled from the city on foot. They carried only blankets and a few other possessions. Bailey Millard watched. *"Never have I seen such a surging tide of humanity as that fighting its way down dusty Bay Street, past the shattered warehouses that had tumbled their heaps of bricks into the road and piled the way with masses of fallen timber,"* he said. In all, hundreds of thousands of people lost their homes. After the quake, they lived in tents in parks, huts, and other temporary structures until the city could be rebuilt.

> " *Fires were blazing in all directions.* "
>
> —Jerome B. Clark,
> a California businessman

A couple prepared a meal at their makeshift camp after the disaster.

Homes tilted and tumbled off their foundations during the quaking.

Measuring Earthquakes

WHEN PEOPLE HEAR THAT AN EARTHQUAKE HAS JUST HAPPENED, THEY WONDER WHERE IT HIT, HOW BIG IT WAS, AND WHETHER ANYONE HAS BEEN HURT. FOR HUNDREDS OF YEARS, PEOPLE HAD NO WAY TO KNOW ALL THE ANSWERS. IF AN EARTHQUAKE KNOCKED BOOKS OFF THE SHELVES IN ONE PLACE, IT MIGHT MEAN A MILD EARTHQUAKE NEARBY. IT ALSO COULD MEAN A GREAT DISASTER HUNDREDS OF MILES AWAY.

For example, Thomas Chase was in downtown San Francisco during the 1906 earthquake. "All morning I worried about my mother and grandmother," he recalled. His home and family were in nearby Oakland, and Tom wanted to know if the damage was worse there. He later learned that his family was fine. Oakland's damage was less severe.

WHERE DID THE EARTH QUAKE?

In modern times, scientists called seismologists study earthquakes. They find the exact location of earthquakes by using seismographs. These instruments use sensors to detect and measure seismic waves. The sensors are so sensitive that they can tell when the ground moves less than the width of a human hair. Seismographs record Earth's shaking in squiggly lines on paper and computer monitors.

A 1980 5.9-magnitude quake toppled bookcases in the library at the Lawrence Livermore National Laboratory nuclear research center in Livermore, California.

28

Sheboygan Falls Schools
Middle School Library
Sheboygan Falls, WI 53085

A California seismologist reads seismograph drums. Scientists use seismographs in groups of three because there are three types of ground movement. The three separate ground motions recorded are up-down, north-south, and east-west.

Thousands of seismographs are used in the United States and around the world. They are in schools, geology research stations, and government buildings. Scientists also have portable seismographs that they can move from place to place.

Many seismographs are connected together into computer networks. They are able to record earthquakes twenty-four hours a day, seven days a week. When an earthquake hits, the seismograph sends instant information on the strength and location over the Internet. The readings from many different locations help scientists learn more about the quake.

To find an earthquake's epicenter, scientists compare when seismic waves reach seismographs in different locations. Scientists need readings from three separate stations to pinpoint the epicenter. The three stations can be thousands of miles away from the epicenter and from one another.

SIZING UP EARTHQUAKES

Seismologists talk about the strength of earthquakes. They use several different scales to determine strength.

In 1935 Charles Richter invented a way to measure and compare the strength of the seismic waves released in a quake. News reports about earthquakes often give the measurement on the Richter scale. People would not notice an earthquake measuring 2.5 on the Richter scale. These little quakes happen every day. A 4.5 quake would shake the ground enough for everyone to notice, and a 6.0 would scare people for miles around. The Richter scale has no maximum number. But the world's biggest recorded quakes have been in the 9s.

DID YOU KNOW?

Seismographs *(below, with Charles Richter)* record Earth's shaking. The strongest recorded earthquake in the world occurred in Chile on May 22, 1960. It measured 9.5 on the Richter scale. The strongest earthquake in the United States hit Alaska on March 28, 1964. It was 9.2 on the Richter scale.

This building crumbled after a 1989 quake
hit California's San Francisco Bay area.

Another scale is called moment magnitude. It measures the amount of rock that broke in a fault after an earthquake and how much the ground moved along the fault. Scientists use this scale more often than the Richter scale because it measures the energy released in a quake. Knowing the energy released provides a better idea of an individual quake's strength. The moment magnitude measurements are similar to Richter measurements. For example, a 1994 earthquake in Northridge, California, was measured at 6.4 on the Richter scale and 6.7 on the moment magnitude scale. This scale also has no maximum number.

For nonscientists, the Modified Mercalli scale often gives the best idea of an earthquake's effects on people, buildings, and other structures. It measures the actual amount of damage at a particular place. It gives a quake's intensity in Roman numerals ranging from I to XII.

BRAINTEASER

Earthquake A was 4.1 on the Richter scale. Earthquake B was 8.1. How much stronger was B?

You might think that B was twice as strong as A. But it was actually 10,000 times stronger. That's because the Richter scale is a logarithmic scale. Every increase of one whole number—from 4.0 to 5.0, for instance—means a quake 10 times stronger. So quake B was really $10 \times 10 \times 10 \times 10$ (10,000 times) stronger than A.

A 1985 quake toppled these buildings in Mexico City, Mexico.

THE MODIFIED MERCALLI SCALE FOR EARTHQUAKE INTENSITY

SCALE	INTENSITY	EFFECT
I	INSTRUMENTAL	NOT FELT BY HUMANS
II	FEEBLE	FELT BY A FEW HUMANS, ESPECIALLY IN UPPER LEVELS OF BUILDINGS
III	SLIGHT	FELT BY MOST PEOPLE INDOORS; HANGING OBJECTS SWING
IV	MODERATE	FELT BY ALMOST EVERYONE; DOORS AND WINDOWS RATTLE
V	SLIGHTLY STRONG	FELT BY EVERYONE; SLIGHT DAMAGE TO POORLY CONSTRUCTED BUILDINGS
VI	STRONG	BOOKS FALL OFF SHELVES; HEAVY FURNITURE MOVES
VII	VERY STRONG	PEOPLE HAVE DIFFICULTY STANDING; WALLS CRACK
VIII	DESTRUCTIVE	DRIVERS HAVE TROUBLE STEERING; CHIMNEYS FALL; TREE BRANCHES BREAK
IX	RUINOUS	GROUND CRACKS; SOME HOUSES COLLAPSE; UNDERGROUND PIPES BREAK; GENERAL PANIC
X	DISASTROUS	LARGE CRACKS IN GROUND; LANDSLIDES COMMON; MANY BUILDINGS DESTROYED
XI	VERY DISASTROUS	MOST BUILDINGS COLLAPSE; SOME BRIDGES DESTROYED; UNDERGROUND PIPELINES DESTROYED
XII	CATASTROPHIC	GROUND MOVES IN WAVES OR RIPPLES; OBJECTS THROWN INTO THE AIR; ALMOST EVERYTHING DESTROYED

May 22, 1960
CHILE

Jose Argomedo, age twenty-two, was riding his horse on Sunday afternoon near Maullin, a town in southern Chile. Suddenly, the ground started shaking so hard that he almost fell off. He jumped down. The ground shook and shook for what seemed like forever.

Argomedo thought it was the start of a nuclear war—that some country had dropped an atomic bomb on Chile. (The United States had dropped two extremely destructive atomic bombs on Japan at the end of World War II in 1945.) Jose was actually living through the start of a magnitude 9.5 earthquake. It was the world's strongest recorded earthquake.

Warning signs had appeared on Saturday, May 21, when many small earthquakes shook the area. Some people were frightened and left their towns. They headed for higher land in the nearby hills, thinking they would be safer there. More small quakes hit the following morning, and people went outside into the streets.

Those small quakes saved many lives. When the big earthquake hit, few people were inside buildings, many of which had collapsed. The quake caused huge landslides, and parts of hillsides and mountainsides came tumbling down. Some landslides dammed up rivers, and the water collected and formed new lakes. The quake killed more than 2,000 people in Chile, injured 3,000, and left about 2 million homeless.

But the quake itself was not the only problem. The earthquake's epicenter was deep under the ocean, about 100 miles (161 km) off the coast of Chile. The quake's seismic waves caused tsunamis that spread through

The force of the 1960 tsunami bent these parking meters in Hilo, Hawaii.

the Pacific Ocean.

One wall of water hit Chile. Vitalia Llanquiman remembered that a man rode by on horseback right after the quake. The rider said something had pulled the water far back from the shore. Vitalia realized that when the sea came back, it might pour onto the land. She and her family ran up a nearby hill to safety.

Another tsunami raced westward across the Pacific. It caused 61 deaths and $75 million in damage in Hilo, Hawaii. When the big waves hit Japan, 138 people died and there was $50 million in damage. Another 32 people died in the Philippines. The wave even caused about $500,000 in damage to the West Coast of the United States.

> "Everyone was terrified as the ground shook. People hugged one another. They screamed and cried."
>
> —Jacqueline de Moras Rosen

People Helping People

AFTER THE GREAT 1755 EARTHQUAKE IN LISBON, PORTUGAL, PEOPLE ASKED, "WHAT NOW?" THE MARQUIS OF POMBAL, WHO HELPED THE KING RULE PORTUGAL, REPLIED, "NOW? WE BURY THE DEAD AND TAKE CARE OF THE LIVING."

Burying the dead and helping the living are still important parts of a community's effort to recover from an earthquake. The survivors need water, food, clothing, and warm blankets. They also need a place to live until new homes can be built. Finding and burying the dead helps to keep diseases from spreading when the dead bodies decay. It also helps relatives and friends to say good-bye to their loved ones.

Wreckage must be cleared away so new buildings can rise up. Workers repair broken water pipes and restore electricity, natural gas, and telephone service. Roads and bridges must be fixed.

NEIGHBORS HELPING NEIGHBORS

Years ago, earthquake victims had to help themselves or rely on help from neighbors. Survivors of the great San Francisco earthquake, for instance, got help from people in nearby Oakland.

AFTERSHOCKS

When the earth stops quaking, people often breathe a sigh of relief. They think the danger has passed. But smaller quakes, known as aftershocks, often follow major shakers. About 15,000 aftershocks followed the 1994 Northridge, California, earthquake. Aftershocks can be a big deal. They may frighten already-fearful survivors. And they can bring down buildings that were damaged by the main quake.

Power shovels cleared the rubble of a collapsed section of the Hanshin Expressway after the 1995 quake in Kobe, Japan.

"There was great activity in Oakland among the people preparing to take care of the thousands of [victims]," recalled Frank Leach, a government worker in Oakland. "Food, bedding, and clothing were provided as if by magic. Thousands of private homes were opened to the sufferers."

Only 100,000 people lived in Oakland. But they cared for about 270,000 people from San Francisco. "Almost everybody in the city of Oakland lent a hand," said F. H. Pratt. "Nobody who entered the city from [San Francisco] was hungry or without a place to sleep."

People depended on local help because transportation was so slow. There were no airplanes to rush aid to the disaster site. Help sent from distant places took days or weeks to arrive by train or horse-drawn wagon.

DISASTER RELIEF WORKERS

Help from neighbors remains important in modern disasters. The government and citizens in the affected state or country do everything they can to help.

In the United States, local fire departments, police, and other emergency personnel arrive at the scene of a disaster first. They give medical help to injured people. Rescue workers also search for people who may be trapped in buildings that have fallen down.

DID YOU KNOW?

Rescue workers use specially trained dogs to sniff out people buried alive beneath the rubble of an earthquake. After the 1988 quake in Armenia (in Western Asia), rescue dogs found more than sixty people buried alive. In Bam, Iran, a ninety-seven-year-old woman was found alive after being buried for eight days in the 2003 earthquake. Another man, age fifty-six, was buried for thirteen days and lived!

A rescue dog sniffed for survivors after a 2001 earthquake and landslide in El Salvador.

Rescue workers attempted to remove people from a toppled building after a quake shook Taipei, Taiwan, in 1999. The quake struck the city while people slept and measured 7.6 on the Richter scale.

Workers from the Federal Emergency Management Agency (FEMA), the American Red Cross, and other organizations help people who have lost their homes.

In other countries, assistance may come from organizations that are part of the International Red Cross and Red Crescent Movement. More help comes from disaster relief teams from other countries and private relief organizations. Within hours of a disaster, these groups can fly in tons of supplies and hundreds of experienced workers. Such help can be especially important in poorer countries, which may not have enough resources to deal with disasters.

"All parts of the world tried to help us," said Anna Mnatsakanyan, who lived in Armenia during the great Spitak earthquake in 1988. "From every country they were sending relief agencies, doctors, Red Cross, volunteers, and many other people . . . to Armenia to help us."

LIQUID GOLD

After an earthquake strikes, water is one of the very first needs. "Water was now more precious than gold, and not a drop must be wasted," said Emma M. Burke, whose home was destroyed during the 1906 San Francisco earthquake.

FEMA IS FOR YOU

Right after a disaster in the United States, FEMA provides some of the most important help. This assistance sometimes includes financial help. FEMA may provide disaster victims with money to start recovering and rebuilding their lives. This money can help repair damages and replace belongings that were destroyed. Some of the money must be paid back, and some is a gift.

A woman carried her water ration after a 1999 quake in Turkey.

A Red Cross worker rescued a twelve-year-old boy. He was trapped for more than thirty-eight hours in rubble created by a 1999 quake in Colombia, South America.

Clean drinking water is especially important. People can go without water for only a short time before they become sick. Without clean water, they would have to drink water from puddles, ponds, and rivers. These sources are often loaded with germs that may cause vomiting, diarrhea, and other health problems.

After the 1995 quake in Kobe, Japan, a student named Fumiko Miyake was without running water for the first time in his life. "I really understand water was the most important material for living creatures," he said. "I also understand how convenient flush toilets had been."

Monty Crisp led a team of relief workers into Bam, Iran, right after a big earthquake in 2003. His team passed out water, shoes, toothpaste, soap, and other supplies.

SURVIVAL KITS

Relief workers often pass out thousands of survival kits. They usually contain a week's worth of food for a family, blankets, and a tent for them to live in.

Sanjay Spjwal, a relief worker at the 2001 earthquake in Gujarat, India, heard firsthand what the people wanted most. "The food is a good thing and we thank you for it," Abdul Hussein told him. "But will you help us rebuild our village?"

HOW TO HELP

Even if you can't help disaster victims in person, you can still support them. Many people donate money to groups that send relief teams and supplies, both inside and out of the United States. The American Red Cross is one of the best-known groups. To find out more, visit its website at http://www.redcross.org. You can also check the U.S. Agency for International Development home page at http://www.usaid.gov. Recent disasters are usually listed in the Features section. The United Nations' ReliefWeb site at http://www.reliefweb.int is another good resource, especially for international disasters.

The Red Cross was on hand to provide supplies to earthquake victims in Los Angeles, California, after a 1994 quake.

Rescue workers entered a collapsed house in India to search for survivors of the 2001 earthquake that rumbled through Gujarat State.

Sometimes rebuilding is impossible. When an earthquake and landslide hit Port Royal, Jamaica, in 1692, two-thirds of the city slid into the Caribbean Sea. More than half of the residents died. Most villages and cities, however, are rebuilt, and life returns to normal.

But even when a town is rebuilt, those who lived through the quake may need more time to recover. Earthquakes are very frightening, and the fear lasts. "I dream that devils are shaking the earth and they are trying to pull me down into it," said nine-year-old Karim Hussein, whose home was destroyed in the Gujarat earthquake in India. "For years following the [1972] Nicaragua earthquake," recalled Gail Meighan, "few people would go to the movies." They were afraid another earthquake would strike, trapping them in the movie theater.

EMOTIONAL RECOVERY

Earthquake survivors don't just have physical needs. They also have emotional needs. Disaster victims often need talk, tears, and time to heal from the shock and stress of their experience.

Talking to friends, family members, and counselors can help people make sense of what has happened. Counselors also help people find ways to return to normal life. In major disasters, teams of specially trained aid workers listen to the survivors and help them grieve and recover. Crying is a natural part of grieving for anyone or anything that has been lost, such as a friend or family member, a pet, or a home. Time gives survivors a chance to move on and begin to rebuild their lives and their communities.

The earthquake in Armenia taught Anna Mnatsakanyan a lesson. "In the world whatever happens like an earthquake, tornado, or a hurricane, no one should lose hope because there is someone that is somewhere that will reach out and help."

> "There are *so many people* who are just *stunned.*"
> —Monty Crisp, after the 2003 quake in Bam, Iran

Survivors of the 2003 earthquake in Bam, Iran, waited for aid outside their ruined homes.

January 17, 1995
KOBE, JAPAN

Fires broke out shortly after the earthquake.

On January 17, 1995, many of the 1.5 million people in Kobe, Japan, were just starting to wake up. At 5:46 A.M., a magnitude 7.2 earthquake hit the city. The intensity was estimated at XII on the Modified Mercalli scale. Kurt Mundt lay in bed and listened to the quake's roar as windows broke, the roof split open, and walls cracked. *"It went on forever,"* he remembered. *"I can't believe it was only 20 seconds."*

In less than half a minute, the great earthquake wrecked much of Kobe. It also damaged nearby towns and cities. *"The whole room was moving around like it was made of jelly,"* said journalist Dennis Kessler. He lived in Osaka, a city of 2.6 million people. *"Every single object in our room was flying around."*

An elevated highway between Kobe and Osaka collapsed in three places. About fifty cars flew off the edge of the road. A bus was left hanging over the edge. Other bridges collapsed all over the area. Trains derailed, and roads twisted and cracked.

Piles of rubble and burned
vehicles littered Kobe
after the earthquake.

Natural gas used for heating and cooking hissed out of broken underground pipes. Sparks set it on fire, and whole areas of Kobe burned down. **"I could see flames licking the sky,"** said Mundt. **"There were far too few firemen and far too little water to stop the fire."** The quake also snapped underground water pipes, making it difficult for firefighters to put out the fires.

Baseball player Ichiro Suzuki was living in Kobe, playing for the pro team Orix Blue Wave. **"I can't put into words how frightening [the earthquake] was,"** he said. When the baseball season began, Ichiro and his teammates wore special patches on their uniforms that read *Gambarou Kobe*, which means "Let's Do Our Best for Kobe!"

" I curled up in my bed and waited to see if I would die. "

—*Kurt Mundt*

More than 6,400 people were killed, and at least 15,000 were injured. The quake left about 50,000 people homeless. It was winter, and the temperature was near freezing. Aid workers set up tents for the people to live in. Even so, the homeless had trouble staying warm.

More than 46,000 buildings were destroyed, including homes, schools, hospitals, stores, and office buildings. The Japanese government rebuilt Kobe, Osaka, and the other damaged areas. The cost of the repairs was close to $100 billion.

Survivors in Kobe gathered
around a pot of food
at an elementary school
used as a shelter.

47

The Future

SCIENTISTS WISH THEY COULD TELL PEOPLE WHEN AN EARTHQUAKE IS ABOUT TO HAPPEN. WE HAVE HURRICANE WARNINGS, TORNADO WARNINGS, AND FLOOD WARNINGS. BUT EARTHQUAKES OFTEN STRIKE WITHOUT WARNING. PREDICTING EARTHQUAKES IS ONE OF THE MAIN GOALS OF SEISMOLOGY, THE STUDY OF SEISMIC WAVES AND EARTHQUAKES.

WHEN? WHERE? HOW BIG?

Seismologists want to know when the next earthquake will occur, where it will happen, and how strong it will be. That information could save many lives.

In 1975 seismologists in China predicted that a big quake soon would occur near Haicheng, a city of 1 million people. Officials evacuated the city. A few days later, a strong earthquake hit. It destroyed much of Haicheng. The prediction and evacuation probably saved 150,000 lives.

Seismologists hoped they had found the secret to predicting earthquakes. But a year later, they failed to predict a quake in Tangshan, China. It killed at least one-quarter of the city's 1 million residents.

Avoiding false alarms also is important. If officials predict an earthquake and nothing happens, people may ignore the next warning—and get caught in a real earthquake.

The 1976 Tangshan quake also damaged buildings in Beijing, China *(above)*. Beijing is about 100 miles (160 km) away from Tangshan.

The 1976 Tangshan earthquake measured 7.8
on the Richter scale. The shocking quake
nearly destroyed the important industrial city.

False alarms have other dangers. They may make thousands of people flee an area very quickly. People may be injured or killed in automobile and other accidents. False alarms also are expensive. People lose time from work and school, and factories, stores, and businesses all shut down.

QUAKE RED FLAGS

The scientists who predicted the Haicheng earthquake noticed warning signs beforehand, including odd animal behavior. Rats appeared dazed, and chickens refused to enter their coops. Perhaps they can sense vibrations or other things that people and instruments cannot detect.

David Jay Brown saw such behavior in a college laboratory in Los Angeles, California. He and several other students were watching three rabbits in the lab. Suddenly the rabbits got excited. "They started hopping around in their cages wildly for around five minutes," he said, "right before a 5.2 earthquake sent the whole building rolling and swaying." Other odd animal behavior before quakes includes fish jumping out of the water, dogs howling in the night, cats hiding, and chickens pecking one another.

Scientists also use instruments to watch for danger signs along earthquake faults. Rocks near faults, for instance, may move slightly before a big slip. Underground stress may make the ground buckle up or sink down. Water levels in wells have changed before some quakes, and certain gases have been released from the ground.

Nothing scientists have found so far is reliable enough to predict that an earthquake will occur during the next week, month, or year. Scientists can only predict the chances that a strong earthquake will occur during the next thirty or fifty years in a specific area. The predictions are based on how often earthquakes happened in the area in the past.

The U.S. Geological Survey (USGS) uses such information to make daily forecasts for small quakes in California. This government agency studies earthquakes. It puts the forecasts online at http://pasadena.wr .usgs.gov/step/.

The remains of a building after the 2001 quake in Bhuj, India. Nearly fifteen thousand people died in the quake, and thousands were left homeless.

GETTING PREPARED

Although people cannot control or predict earthquakes, they can take actions that will reduce the deaths, injuries, and destruction. Being prepared is especially important for people living where earthquakes often occur.

The most important steps involve making sure that homes, offices, schools, bridges, and other structures are built to withstand severe shaking. Earthquake-resistant buildings are designed to flex or bend but not break apart when the shaking begins.

Some buildings sit on thick rubber pads or springs that act as shock absorbers. Earthquake-resistant buildings and bridges also have extra beams and supports. Those supports tie the walls, floor, roof, and foundations together into a boxlike shape. They help the structure survive the side-to-side shaking during a quake.

Many earthquake-prone areas have laws requiring that buildings be earthquake resistant. These types of buildings can save many lives.

DROP, COVER, HOLD ON!

People need to know what to do when the shaking begins. The American Red Cross advises people to stay indoors until the shaking stops and you are sure it is safe to exit. Stay away from windows because they may break. Buildings in the United States are stronger than those in places like Bam, Iran, and do give some protection.

AND TOTO, TOO

In case a disaster strikes, keep an emergency kit at home and in each vehicle. Include a flashlight and spare batteries, a battery-powered radio and spare batteries, some water and food, and a first-aid kit. And remember your pets! Include pet food and water in plastic bottles. A leash or harness and a pet carrier may also help. And you'll need a photo of your cat or dog in case your pet gets lost.

EARTHQUAKE-PROOF BUILDING

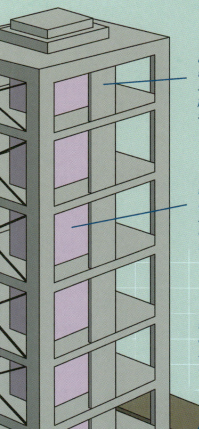

CROSS-BRACING
helps stabilize buildings from the side-to-side shaking of an earthquake.

SHEAR WALLS
are vertical walls that make a building's frame stiffer. They help the frame resist side-to-side shaking.

A SHEAR CORE
is in the center of a building. It often surrounds elevators or stairs. It is similar to shear walls.

BRACE ISOLATORS
sit between a building's bottom floor and the foundation (base). They reduce building shaking during a quake.

A MOAT
is an empty space around a building's base. It allows the building to sway during a quake.

Pick a safe place in every room. It might be under a strong table or desk or against an inside wall where nothing can fall on you. Then practice Drop, Cover, and Hold On at least twice a year. Drop to the ground. Take cover by getting under a sturdy table or other piece of furniture. Hold on until the shaking stops.

If you're in bed and you feel an earthquake, hold on. Protect your head with a pillow. If you are outdoors, find a clear spot away from buildings, trees, and electric power lines.

A Japanese girl ducked under her desk during an earthquake drill at her elementary school.

Then drop to the ground. If you're in a car, slow down and drive to a clear spot. Stay away from highway bridges and stay in the car until the shaking stops. Knowing how to prepare for an earthquake and what to do when the shaking starts is very important. The knowledge can save lives and protect family members, friends, and pets.

STAYING SAFE

If you live in an earthquake danger zone, you and your family can do several things to stay safe. Make sure the family has an emergency plan and keeps an emergency kit on hand. You can also search your house for hazards before a quake strikes.

- Fasten bookcases, mirrors, and other display cases to the wall so they will not fall.

- Move heavy objects on shelves to the bottom shelf or fasten them to the shelf.

- Lock the wheels on any rolling TV carts so the cart cannot roll.

- If your bed is next to a window, move it away from the window.

- Move any heavy pictures so they're not hanging above a bed.

- Install latches on cabinet doors so that the doors will stay closed.

Timeline

A.D. *526* An earthquake near Antioch, Syria, kills approximately 250,000 people.

856 A quake near Damghan, Iran, kills 200,000.

1556 The deadliest quake ever recorded kills 830,000 people near Shenshi Province in China.

1692 A shaker causes parts of Port Royal, Jamaica, to slide into the ocean.

1755 In an earthquake that destroys most of the city, more than 90,000 residents of Lisbon, Portugal, are killed.

1811 Earthquakes in New Madrid, Missouri *(right)*, change the course of the Mississippi River.

1906 The great San Francisco earthquake and subsequent fire destroy much of the city.

1908 A quake totally destroys Messina, Italy, and kills between 70,000 and 100,000 people.

1935 Working in California, Charles Richter develops a way to measure earthquake strength.

1960 The strongest earthquake ever recorded—9.5 on the Richter scale—hits Chile in South America.

1964 The strongest-ever quake in North America—9.2 on the Richter scale—strikes Anchorage, Alaska *(left),* and surrounding areas.

1972 Managua, Nicaragua, is devastated by a quake that kills at least 5,000 people.

1976 The worst earthquake to hit China in the twentieth century leaves almost 300,000 people dead.

1988 In Armenia a quake kills at least 25,000 people and leaves 500,000 people homeless.

1989 The Loma Prieta earthquake *(left)* strikes San Francisco, California, just before Game Three of the World Series (between the San Francisco Giants and the Oakland Athletics) begins. The game is canceled.

1994 In Northridge, California, an earthquake kills 57 and causes $80 billion in damage.

1995 Kobe, Japan, is struck with a 7.2 quake, which causes more than $100 billion in damage.

1998 Two quakes devastate northern Afghanistan.

1999 Strong earthquakes cause great damage in Colombia and Turkey *(right)*.

2001 About 600,000 people are left homeless by a severe quake in Bhuj, India.

2003 After the Bam, Iran, earthquake, 26,000 are dead and at least 10,000 are injured.

2004 An earthquake off the coast of Sumatra, Indonesia, creates a devastating tsunami in the Indian Ocean that kills more than 150,000 people.

2005 A devastating earthquake strikes parts of Pakistan *(left)*, India, and Afghanistan, killing more than 80,000 people.

Glossary

aftershock: smaller earthquakes that come after a large quake

body wave: a seismic wave that travels through Earth's interior

crust: the outermost layer of Earth

earthquake: a shaking of Earth's surface caused by movements of underground rock

epicenter: the point on Earth's surface directly above the point where an earthquake occurred

evacuate: to leave a dangerous area and go somewhere safe

hypocenter: the point underground at which an earthquake began

Modified Mercalli scale: a scale for measuring earthquakes based on how much damage they cause

moment magnitude: a scale for measuring earthquakes based on how much energy they release

Richter scale: a scale for measuring earthquakes based on the strength of seismic waves

Ring of Fire: the region where Earth's tectonic plates meet. Many earthquakes take place in this area, which stretches around the Pacific Ocean from North and South America to Asia.

seismic waves: vibrations in the ground produced by earthquakes

seismograph: an instrument that records movements of the ground, or seismic waves

seismologist: a scientist who studies earthquakes

surface wave: a seismic wave that travels along Earth's surface

tectonic plates: huge chunks of rock that carry Earth's continents and oceans. Earthquakes result from movement by these plates.

tsunami: a large ocean wave produced by an underwater earthquake, a volcanic eruption, or a landslide

Places to Visit

Many museums have exhibits about earthquakes. Check the websites of museums close to you for hours of operation and other information.

Carnegie Science Center in Pittsburgh, Pennsylvania
http://www.carnegiesciencecenter.org.
Visit the Forces of Nature Exhibit in the SciQuest gallery, and feel the seismic waves of three different earthquakes.

Lawrence Hall of Science in Berkeley, California
http://www.lhs.berkeley.edu/exhibits/exhibitsmore.html.
Visit the permanent exhibit on earthquakes, and see a real seismograph.

San Andreas Fault
Several companies offer guided tours of the most famous earthquake fault. Search the Internet for "tour San Andreas Fault."

Santa Ana Discovery Science Center in Santa Ana, California
http://www.discoverycube.org
Visit the Quake Zone and the Shake Shack to experience a 6.4 tremor!

Valdez, Alaska
http://www.alaska.net/~vldzmuse/oldtown1.htm
The city was severely damaged by a 1964 earthquake. This museum has a model of the original town as it existed before the earthquake.

Virtual Museum of the City of San Francisco
http://www.sfmuseum.org/
This museum, devoted to the 1906 quake and fire, is just a few seconds away from you. It's an online museum.

Source Notes

4   "Girl, Five, Recalls Kashmir Quake," *BBC News,* October 12, 2005 http://news.bbc.co.uk/go/pr/fr/-/1/hi/world/south_asia/4333592.stm (December 24, 2005).

4   "'The Cries of Those Trapped Haunt Me'" *BBC News,* October 8, 2005 http://news.bbc.co.uk/go/pr/fr/-/1/hi/world/south_asia/4322496.stm (December 24, 2005).

4   Ibid.

5   Till Mayer, "South Asia Quake: Death in the Mountains," *CNN.com,* October 18, 2005 http://www.cnn.com/2005/WORLD/asiapcf/10/18/quake.redcross/ (January 10, 2006).

5   "Eyewitness: Kashmir Earthquake," *BBC News,* October 10, 2005 http://news.bbc.co.uk/1/hi/world/south_asia/4323060.stm (January 10, 2006).

8   Charles Kendrick, "The Great Disaster," *The Virtual Museum of the City of San Francisco,* n.d., http://www.sfmuseum.net/1906/ew17.html (September 22, 2005).

9   Gail Meighan, in e-mail to authors, July 2005.

11 Rev. Charles Davy, "The Earthquake at Lisbon, 1755," *Modern History Sourcebook,* November 1998, http://www.fordham.edu/halsall/mod/1755lisbonquake.html (September 23, 2005).

11 Ibid.

17 LeAnne Katz, in e-mail to authors, July 2005.

20 "The Day the Mississippi Ran Backward," *State Emergency Management Agency,* n.d., http://www.sema.state.mo.us/backward.htm (September 23, 2005).

20 Eliza Bryan, "The New Madrid Earthquake," *The Virtual Times,* n.d., http://hsv.com/genlintr/newmadrd/accnt1.htm (September 23, 2005).

21 George Heinrich Crist, "The New Madrid Earthquake," *The Virtual Times,* n.d., http://hsv.com/genlintr/newmadrd/accnt3.htm (September 23, 2005).

26 Charles B. Sedgwick, "The Fall of San Francisco: Some Personal Observations," *The Virtual Museum of the City of San Francisco,* n.d., http://www.sfmuseum.net/1906.2/ew20.html (September 22, 2005).

26–27 Ibid.

27 Bailey Millard, "Thousands Flee from Blazing City," *The Virtual Museum of the City of San Francisco,* n.d., http://www.sfmuseum.net/1906/ew12.html (September 23, 2005).

27 "The San Francisco Earthquake, 1906," *EyeWitness to History.com,* n.d., http://www.eyewitnesstohistory.com/sfeq.htm (September 23, 2005).

28 Thomas Chase, "Thomas Chases Eyewitness Account at the Ferry Building," *The Virtual Museum of the City of San Francisco,* n.d., http://www.sfmuseum.net/1906/ew1.html (September 23, 2005).

35 Jacqueline de Moras Rosen, personal interview with authors, October 6, 2004.

36 "1755 Lisbon Earthquake: The Day After," *Wikiverse.org,* n.d., http://1755-lisbon-earthquake.wikiverse.org/ (September 23, 2005).

38 Frank Leach, "Great Earthquake and Fire of 1906," *The Virtual Museum of the City of San Francisco,* n.d., http://www.sfmuseum.net/1906.2/ew22.html (September 23, 2005).

38 F. H. Pratt "Alameda Building Trades Relief Work," *The Virtual Museum of the City of San Francisco,* n.d., http://www.sfmuseum.net/1906.2/oakland.html (September 23, 2005).

40 Anna Mnatsakanyan, "Anna Mnatsakanyan: Her Unforgettable Nightmare," *clarkhumanities.org,* n.d., http://www.clarkhumanities.org/block3/0324.htm (September 23, 2005).

40 Emma M. Burke, "Comprehending the Calamity," *The Virtual Museum of the City of San Francisco,* n.d., http://www.sfmuseum.net/1906/ew13.html (September 23, 2005).

42 Fumiko Miyake, "The Earthquake," *Kobe University Cross Cultural Studies English Composition Project,* n.d., http://ccs.cla.kobe-u.ac.jp/Asia/Visitor/Furm/report/miyake.html (September 23, 2005).

42 John Schenk, "Quake Zone and Apocalyptic Landscape," World Vision Communications, February 3, 2001, http://www.worldvision.org/worldvision/virtual.nsf.stable/helpquakevictims_reports!OpenDocument (August 2004).

44 Ibid.

44 Gail Meighan, in e-mail to authors, July 2005.

44 Mnatsakanyan, *clarkhumanities.org.*

45 Monty Crisp, "Iran Earthquake Response Updated 13 Jan 2004," *ReliefWeb,* January 13, 2004, http://www.reliefweb.int/rw/rwb.nsf/0/1b1916bcf6f6740485256e1b005bc8c9?OpenDocument (September 23, 2005).

46 Kurt Mundt, "Kobe's Hanshin Earthquake–Eyewitness Account," *paulzilla.org,* January 31, 1995, http://www.paulzilla.org/japanese/quakkurt.htm (September 23, 2005).

46 "1995: Earthquake Devastates Kobe," *BBC News,* n.d., http://news.bbc.co.uk/onthisday/hi/dates/stories/january/17/newsid_3375000/3375733.stm (September 23, 2005).

47 Mundt, *paulzilla.org.*

47 Narumi Komatsu, *Ichiro on Ichiro: Interviews with Narumi Komatsu,* translated by Philip Gabriel (Tokyo: Shinchosha Publishing, 2002), 141.

47 Mundt, *paulzilla.org.*

50 David Jay Brown, "Etho-Geological Forecasting: Unusual Animal Behavior & Earthquake Prediction," *Levity.com,* n.d., http://www.levity.com/mavericks/quake.htm (September 23, 2005).

Selected Bibliography

Brumbaugh, David S. *Earthquakes: Science and Society*. Upper Saddle River, NJ: Prentice Hall, 1999.

Davis, Lee. *Natural Disasters*. New York: Facts on File, 2002.

Hancock, Paul L., and Brian J. Skinner, eds. *The Oxford Companion to the Earth*. New York: Oxford University Press, 2000.

Hough, Susan Elizabeth. *Earthshaking Science: What We Know (and Don't Know) about Earthquakes*. Princeton, NJ: Princeton University Press, 2002.

Kurzman, Dan. *Disaster!: The Great San Francisco Earthquake and Fire of 1906*. New York: William Morrow, 2001.

McGuire, Bill. *Raging Planet: Earthquakes, Volcanoes, and the Tectonic Threat to Life on Earth*. Hauppage, NY: Barron's, 2002.

Prager, Ellen. *Furious Earth: The Science and Nature of Earthquakes, Volcanoes and Tsunamis*. New York: McGraw-Hill, 2000.

Ritchie, David. *Encyclopedia of Earthquakes and Volcanoes*. New York: Facts on File, 2001.

Further Resources

BOOKS

Barnard, Bryn. *Dangerous Planet: Natural Disasters That Changed History*. New York: Crown Publishers, 2003. Find out how ten big natural disasters changed the course of history, including a possible meteorite that wiped out the dinosaurs.

Chambers, Catherine. *Earthquakes*. Chicago: Heinemann Library, 2001. This is one of a series of six books that describes weather disasters and how scientists predict and measure them.

Enderle, Judith Ross. *Francis, the Earthquake Dog*. San Francisco: Chronicle Books, 1996. Read the story of the terrier found in the basement of the St. Francis Hotel after the 1906 San Francisco earthquake.

George, Linda. *Plate Tectonics*. San Diego: Kidhaven Press, 2003. Read about how the continents float on big plates of rock, the Ring of Fire, and the theory of plate tectonics.

Kehret, Peg. *Earthquake Terror*. New York: Cobblehill Books/Dutton, 1996. Jonathan must find a way to save himself and his handicapped sister from an earthquake that strikes their summer camp.

Maslin, Mark. *Restless Planet: Earthquakes*. Austin, TX: Raintree Steck-Vaughn, 2000. Learn about the relief and rescue efforts after earthquake disasters.

Nicolson, Cynthia Pratt. *Earthquake*. Toronto: Kids Can Press, 2001. *Earthquake* provides basic information about the dramatic effects of earthquakes and provides diagrams and maps with captions.

Prager, Ellen J. *Earthquakes*. Washington, DC: National Geographic Society, 2002. Enjoy a bird's-eye view of an earthquake, and then learn about plate tectonics.

Rogers, Daniel. *Earthquakes*. Austin, TX: Raintree Steck-Vaughn, 1999. Great basic information on earthquakes is included in this book, as well as methods of measurement and aftershocks.

Simon, Seymour. *Danger! Earthquakes*. New York: Seastar Books, 2002. Learn about the dynamics of earthquakes and how to survive a quake.

Sutherland, Lin. *Earthquakes and Volcanoes*. Pleasantville, NY: Reader's Digest Children's Books, 2000. This book offers clear and concise explanations of the geological processes that cause earthquakes.

Van Rose, Susanna. *Eyewitness Books: Volcano & Earthquake*. New York: Knopf, 1992. Colorful photographs and drawings help explain the magnitude and destruction of earthquakes around the world.

Walker, Sally M. *Earthquakes*. Minneapolis: Carolrhoda Books, Inc., 1996. This book explains, in simple terms, how earthquakes are measured and predicted.

Woods, Michael, and Mary B. Woods. *Tsunamis*. Minneapolis: Lerner Publications Company, 2007. Find out more about some of the world's most destructive tsunamis.

WEBSITES AND FILMS

ABAG Earthquake Info—Kids Zone
http://www.abag.ca.gov/bayarea/eqmaps/kids.html
Take a quiz, and test your earthquake knowledge.

American Red Cross
http://www.redcross.org/services/disaster
The Red Cross, famous for its disaster relief programs, offers a bounty of practical information, including precautions and supplies for surviving earthquakes.

Earthquake!
http://www.nationalgeographic.com/ngkids/0403
Follow a slide presentation that shows earthquake damage and gives safety advice.

Earthquake Facts
http://www.ceri.memphis.edu/public/
The University of Memphis's Center for Earthquake Research and Information is packed with practical information on preparing for and surviving quakes.

Earthquakes
http://edtech.kennesaw.edu/web/earthqu.html
Fun links by the dozen are at this wonderful website from Kennesaw State University for kids, parents, and teachers.

FEMA for KIDS Homepage
http://www.fema.gov/kids
The Federal Emergency Management Agency offers kid-friendly information and safety tips about earthquakes and other disasters.

Understanding Earthquakes
http://crustal.ucsb.edu/ics/understanding
A revolving globe shows you the location of the biggest earthquakes in the last five years. You'll also find famous earthquake accounts and a quiz.

USGS Earthquake Hazards Program
http://earthquake.usgs.gov
You will find everything anyone could ever want to know about earthquakes, plus great links to more sites for kids.

All About Earthquakes. Wynnewood, PA: Schlessinger Video Production, 2000. In this video, learn about earthquakes and the instruments that are used to measure them.

The Case of the Shaky Quake. Washington, DC: NASA, 2002. The child detectives feel the effects of an earthquake and search for information about plate tectonics.

The Great San Francisco Earthquake, 1906. Alexandria, VA: PBS Video, 1988. You can view seldom-seen footage of the incredible San Francisco earthquake of 1906 and hear the stories of the survivors who rebuilt the city in three years.

NOVA: Explorations in Earth Science: Earthquake. Boston: WGBH, 1990. NOVA produced this video after the 1989 Loma Prieta earthquake in California.

Index

Photo Acknowledgments

The photos in this book are used with the permission of: Andrea Booher/FEMA, p. 1; Robert A. Eplett/FEMA, pp. 3, 17; © FAROOQ NAEEM/AFP/Getty Images, p. 4; © ERIC FEFERBERG/AFP/Getty Images, p. 5; © Karl Grobl/ZUMA Press, p. 7; © Bettmann/CORBIS, pp. 9, 30, 34, 35, 48, 49; © Time Life Pictures/Mansell/Time Life Pictures/Getty Images, pp. 10, 11; © Tom Bean/CORBIS, p. 13; FEMA, pp. 15, 55; © Todd Strand/ Independent Picture Service, p. 16; Earth Science Photographic Archive, U.S. Geological Survey Photo Library, pp. 18, 20, 21 (top), 31, 53, 57 (top); © Roger Ressmeyer/CORBIS, p. 19; © Raymond Gehman/CORBIS, p. 21 (bottom); Kevin Galvin/FEMA, p. 22; © Paula Bronstein/Getty Images, p. 23; National Archives, p. 26; Library of Congress, p. 27 (LC-DIG-ppmsca-09835, left; LC-DIG-ppmsca-09834, right); Courtesy of the National Oceanic and Atmospheric Administration, pp. 28, 56 (bottom); © Vince Streano/CORBIS, p. 29; © Nik Wheeler/ CORBIS, p. 33; © Michael S. Yamashita/CORBIS, pp. 37, 47 (both); © Reuters/CORBIS, pp. 38, 39, 41, 54; © LE SEGRETAIN PASCAL/CORBIS SYGMA, p. 40; © Joseph Sohm; ChromoSohm Inc./CORBIS, p. 42; © Kapoor Baldev/Sygma/CORBIS, p. 43; © Shahpari Sohaie/CORBIS, p. 45; © Patrick Robert/Sygma/CORBIS, p. 46; © TC Malhotra/ZUMA Press, p. 51; © Sam Lund/Independent Picture Service, p. 52; © North Wind/ North Wind Picture Archives, p. 56 (top); © Mark Milstein/ZUMA Press, p. 57 (center); © Chris Stowers/ JiwaFoto/ZUMA Press, p. 57 (bottom). Diagrams by Bill Hauser, pp. 15, 33, 53.

Front Cover: © AP/Wide World Photos; Back Cover: Earth Science Photographic Archive, U.S. Geological Survey Photo Library.

About the Authors

Michael Woods is a science and medical journalist in Washington, D. C., who has won many national writing awards. He works in the Washington Bureau of the *Pittsburgh Post-Gazette* and the *Toledo Blade*. Mary B. Woods has been a librarian in the Fairfax County Public School System in Virginia and the Benjamin Franklin International School in Barcelona, Spain. The Woodses' other books include the eight-volume Ancient Technology series. The Woodses have four children. When not writing, reading, or enjoying their grandchildren, they travel to gather material for future books.